It's About More Than Just The Gear:

Examining the overlooked aspects of preparedness.

By Shawn Clay

Introduction by Dr. David Powers

Table of Contents

Disclaimer

The advice and recommendations given in this book are purely for informational purposes only. When making any lifestyle changes, be it physical, financial, emotional, etc., please consult a professional in that field for advice. The opinions stated in this book are that of the author and not intended to be taken as professional advice.

Introduction

In my occupation and my hobbies, I meet a lot of preppers and self-reliant folks. At least, that's what many of them call themselves. They all prep in one way or another, and almost all of those people I know over-prep in at least one area, to the detriment of most other areas.

Some of them have tons of guns and ammo, but not much food.

I know of at least one that has a lot of everything, but he lives in a trailer park as his retreat property.

Some have beautiful gardens and food stores, but few weapons.

I see quite a few that have a little of everything, except no medicine stores.

Some have way too many knives, but no skills.

And then there's my favorite...

I really get a kick out of it when I meet the special prepper-type who has tons of food stored just right, pallets of ammo in specific calibers for the weapons he owns, back up clothes to last for years, his electronics stored in Faraday bags and boxes, and all the right skills to create food, weapons, and even homemade alcohol.

But…

The poor guy is in such bad shape that he's likely to die of a heart attack the first week of an adverse situation, or die of diabetes the first month of the apocalypse, or he just plain old ignored *Zombieland's* survival rule number one, which is C-A-R-D-I-O, and he's gonna get eaten by one of those really slow zombies with no legs that's crawling after him, and he still can't outrun it.

I pay attention to those guys because when they croak, I'll bury them, pray over the grave, and give them a hearty thanks for all the supplies.

Don't be that guy. Don't get me wrong: I do want the supplies, but I'd rather you help me survive the apocalypse as a friend than as a link in my supply chain.

This book is all about helping you to not be that guy. My main prepper pet peeve is health and fitness, but this guide covers so much more. The author delves into all the necessary areas you need to pay attention to in order to survive the end of the world, or at least the next bad weather incident. You can be like most preppers and complete your list of goodies by storing and stockpiling all the right things, but you need to know that there are things you won't find on any Bug Out Bag list. There are some things that take time, assistance, or both. You better pay attention to what Shawn Clay has to say in this guide and get started.

If you don't pay attention, go ahead and send me your address. I want to be first in line for your stuff.

Dr. David Powers

Dr. David Powers is an adventurer, philosopher, and pioneer. He is considered an expert in team building and goal setting and having perfected these skills in life-threatening situations, now teaches them in conferences and other settings.

He is a best-selling author in cognitive psychology and experimental education. He is a decorated veteran of the Marine Corps and a founding member of the U.S. Department of Homeland Security. He is married and the proud father of three feral boys and one princess that he and his wife homeschool. His mission in life is to find the magical best mug of coffee in the world.

Be sure to check him out at CallSignRedbeard.com.

Chapter 1: It's about more than just the gear.

If you are even remotely familiar with the concept of prepping, you no doubt realize that there is an endless amount of gear that is associated with the lifestyle. Bug out bags, freeze dried foods, water filters, first aid kits, radios, survival guides.....the list of goods available is endless. Every day of the week, I know that I personally get multiple emails, catalogs, and social media posts about the newest and latest survival gear that I simply MUST have. While some of this gear is definitely useful, the majority is mass-produced and of questionable quality. A seasoned prepper knows that a lot of gear is designed to be appealing to the eye, similar to how some fishing lures are designed more to capture the attention of a fisherman rather than to catch an actual fish.

Now that prepping has gone much more mainstream in modern society, there are entire industries devoted to manufacturing and marketing their wares to an ever-increasing demographic. The days of only having the local Army surplus store available for all your needs is long gone. Brick and mortar storefronts, as well as a slew of online stores, now cater to the prepping lifestyle. From pre-packaged bug out bags to abandoned missile silos repurposed into bunkers, there is no shortage of ways to empty one's wallet in a hurry.

While gear is certainly a major focus of any prepper's lifestyle, it cannot be the sole driver behind the movement. All the gear in the world will not help you if you do not have several additional skills to go along with it. The purpose of this book is to outline some of the various tenets of prepping that are vital to the lifestyle, yet are often overlooked as we chase after the newest addition to our bug out bags.

It's my hope that this book will open the eyes of the beginning prepper that there is a whole world that lies just beyond the stack of gear in the closet. I also hope that it serves as a reminder to the seasoned prepper that skills are the cornerstone of the prepping lifestyle. Our ancestors weathered tough times with much less than we have available to us. The difference was, they valued resourcefulness, skills, and ingenuity more than "stuff". We would be well advised to learn from their example.

Now, I know that talking about aspects of prepping other than the latest survival knife or the never ending debate about the best bugout weapon may be considered as much fun as having to read the instruction manual before operating that new device you just bought, but give this book a chance. It just might open your eyes to how much you've been missing out on! The well-rounded prepper knows that what lies between the ears is just as important as what is packed in the bag.

Chapter 2: Functional Preparation

Back when I was in my late teens, I had a lifted 1977 Ford F150 4x4 with some of the most extreme mud tires you've ever laid your eyes on. It was huge, ugly, and got about 3 gallons to the mile, but it was my pride and joy. There was no mud hole that could stop it. One summer day, I drove over to the local gas station near my house to fill it up. The owner's son was running the place that day and asked me if I would like to make some quick money. He said that they had a call for a wrecker to come pull out a stuck SUV over at an area near some government land where all the locals went to go four-wheeling and mud bogging. He said that he wasn't sure that the station's 2 wheel drive tow truck could make it out to where the vehicle was stuck, due to some recent rains that made it even harder to get in and out. I told him that was fine with me and after tossing some tow straps and chains into the back of my truck, we were off to pull this poor sap out of the mud.

Upon arriving at the scene, we could clearly see a brand new Nissan Pathfinder stuck nearly up to the windows in a mud hole. The owner, a 16 year-old kid, had climbed out the window and had been jamming limbs, rocks, and whatever other kind of debris he could find in a vain attempt to give his tires some traction, but it was obvious he was in way over his head. My friend had the boy's mother (who was riding shotgun) sign a liability waiver and then hooked up a strap to the trailer hitch of his SUV. We secured the strap to my trailer hitch and in less than 30 seconds, we had him free from his muddy tomb.

When we got him loose, we noticed (in addition to the temporary tag that the dealer had attached only hours before) that he had stock street tires on his vehicle and my buddy advised him that if he was going to be engaging in some hard-core mud bogging, he might consider running a tire that was a tad bit more aggressive than what could be found on a Nissan minivan. The kid had not even considered this, let alone a suspension lift, recovery equipment, or any other accessories that would have properly outfitted him for his adventures. He told us that he just put it in 4 wheel drive and took off into the muddy trails. I think he made it all of about 75 feet before burying it.

I'm sure it's fairly clear what the moral of the story is here: just because the kid had a nice, fancy, 4 wheel drive SUV didn't mean he was ready to be the next mud bog winner. He had made multiple mistakes before ever arriving at the trail head. Improper vehicle setup, improper approach to the obstacles, lack of recovery gear, etc. My buddy made it clear to him and his mother that had they been somewhere more remote, they likely would have been walking home minus a $30k SUV.

Of course, the mere presence of gear doesn't necessarily guarantee a different outcome. Not long after the above experience, I got a call one evening from a friend of mine. He was in a complete panic and stuck in yet another mud hole. The difference was, he was in his father's newly-restored 1985 Chevrolet Silverado 4x4, complete with a 10k pound Warn winch and bumper. The problem was, the solenoid in the winch motor decided to burn up after my buddy ran out about 60 feet of cable around the nearest large tree and tried to start pulling himself out. He had managed to disconnect the cable and wrapped it around the bumper of the truck and decided it was time to call for help. Oh, it should also be mentioned that his father was out of town at the time and he was under strict orders not to drive the truck.

I was at work at the time and couldn't go help him. Long story short, he wound up having to call an after-hours towing company with a 4 wheel drive wrecker to come bail him out. He was able to mostly clean up the truck before his father got back home, but the cable-wrapped front bumper gave him away as soon as his dad pulled into the driveway. Needless to say, in addition to the parental consequences, he was also out the money for the towing bill, which I believe was measured in hundreds of dollars.

The reason for my trips down memory lane is to illustrate two very important points. First of all, going at something blindly, with little to no preparation is a recipe for disaster. Secondly, just because you have the right gear is no guarantee that Murphy won't sneak in and completely ruin your day.

The correlation between these stories and the prepping world should be quite obvious. In the matter of the first point, how many of us know people who have bought one of those ready-made "survival kits", tossed it into the closet, and go about their day feeling like they are ready to survive Armageddon? In regards to the second point, how many of us know people who drive off the lot in a truck or SUV that looks like it belongs in the next Terminator movie, yet have no idea how to even engage the 4 wheel drive setting?

It's easy to see how important it is to have practical, functional knowledge to go along with all that gear we all have. Without it, we have closets, backpacks, and driveways full of fancy paperweights. Some people, especially those in the beginning stages of prepping, tend to focus so much time, effort, and money into buying the right "stuff" that they tend to overlook the fact that they need to know how to use it, both properly and safely.

When it comes to everyone's favorite topic, bug out bags, some of the most experienced survivalists have recommended that you grab your bag one weekend, head out the door, and survive overnight on just the contents. The merits of this exercise should be fairly obvious. In this trial run, you will quickly learn that you need to know how to use that ferro rod, water filter, etc. Hopefully, you have educated yourself on each purchase as you obtained them, but a dry run of your evacuation plan is always a good idea to put that instructional knowledge to work. It also allows one to identify the items in their pack that are not as necessary as they thought, while highlighting all the things that they wish they had packed instead. It's truly better to learn in conditions such as this, as opposed to when the SHTF and there is no time to think, just time to act.

Know how to assemble, disassemble, and perform maintenance on any gear that has moving parts. If there are parts that are susceptible to breakage, I would encourage purchasing and carrying spares, along with knowing how to remove and replace any broken or damaged parts. Like the person on the side of the road who is simply staring into their trunk at the spare tire and jack, don't be the person who has the spare parts, but has no idea what to do with them.

When it comes to shelter, do you know how to set up that ultralight backpacking tent you bought from REI? Can you do it at night, in the rain, or during some other stressful event? Can you take it down and repack it without extra parts left over? Should your tent be rendered unusable, do you have a backup plan for shelter?

When it comes to cooking and food, do you know how to set up and properly use that tiny stove and fuel canister? Do you have adequate cooking gear? Again, a time of distress is not the time to find out that you are woefully unprepared.

When it comes to first aid, do you know what to do for a cut or laceration? What about insect or animal bite? Broken bone or sprain? Shock? Hypothermia or heat stroke? You may find that your $10 first aid kit from Walgreens is not exactly stocked for your needs.

While it may seem overwhelming to consider all the skills and knowledge that seem to be necessary in order to be a well-rounded prepper, one need not despair. Rome wasn't built in a day, and neither will your prepping lifestyle. The good news is, you don't have to go it alone. A quick online or Facebook search will probably show you prepper blogs and probably even a prepper group or store near you that offers classes on all the topics I have discussed, plus many more. In my hometown of Chattanooga, Tennessee, there is a wonderful store called P5 Preparedness that not only sells all the gear necessary to embrace the prepper lifestyle, they also offer classes on every prepping topic under the sun. The staff there are very passionate about the preparedness lifestyle and are willing and eager to teach those who are ready to learn. If you are in the mountains of North Carolina, I would heartily recommend a trip to Carolina Readiness Supply. They are a one stop shop for all things prepping. All the questions about gear, usage, maintenance, pack selection, etc. can be answered by a place like this.

Online, stores such as Emergency Essentials sometimes have blogs that are helpful and cover a wide variety of prepping topics as well. I would encourage any prepper, new or seasoned, to find locals that are of the same mindset and connect with them. Not only will you be able to compare gear and methods, but you will likely form ties that may be beneficial in the future.

I would offer a word of caution about simply heading to a big box sporting goods retailer and raiding the camping aisle. While places like this are great for seeing what all is available, often times the employee manning the department may not exactly have the necessary knowledge and experience to help you make wise decisions. While some retail outlets do a wonderful job of placing passionate personnel in their areas of expertise, you will more likely find that the person behind the counter may have been working in the shoe section the week before. Not exactly the person I want recommending gear that my life may depend on. Not only would I seek the advice of a seasoned prepper or a dedicated store over that of the 18 year-old behind the gun counter at Wal-mart, there are also a ton of videos online on You Tube and other sites that can help you with your prepping needs and questions. As with the retail outlets, some of these videos border on moronic, but I would start out watching videos from respected people in the preparedness field. To start with, Alan Kay, the season 1 winner from History Channel's series Alone, has an excellent video available on You Tube (https://www.youtube.com/watch?v=Tk-r-X1i5i8) about the contents of his personal bugout bag. He breaks down the purpose and function of every component. I highly recommend that, regardless of your prepping status, you watch it. I guarantee you will come away with something new. He also has a website (http://alankaysurvival.com/) with a ton of useful information.

For other skills, such as first aid, consider community or government resources that are available. The Red Cross offers first aid and CPR certification classes all the time all across the nation. I can attest that the classes are well-taught, practical, and presented in a way that holds one's interest. In a few hours, you can be armed with the skills to deal with the majority of medical issues that you may encounter. I highly recommend them. I would also check out your local or state emergency management agency, as well as FEMA. Some locations have weekend workshops, while agencies such as FEMA have online classes on emergency management and other SHTF topics. This is continuing education that can certainly pay off in droves if you ever need that knowledge in an emergency situation.

Functional knowledge can also extend into the more mundane aspects of being prepared. For instance, do you know how to change the tire on your vehicle? Can you perform basic maintenance on it should you have to be your own mechanic? Can you refuel from fuel cans if the gas stations around you are out of power or fuel? Do you know how to read a basic road map if the cell towers are down and your GPS on your phone is no longer reliable? Do you know how to drive in adverse weather conditions such as snow, ice, and heavy rain? Again, these are issues that need to be addressed long before an event happens. In many cases, the knowledge may be essential just to get yourself or your family home safely.

In your home, do you know how to turn off the main power source? If you are on natural gas, do you know where the valve to shut off the feed is located? How about the main water intake? In the event of a major storm, you may have to quickly shut these items off if your home is compromised. Do you have the skills and supplies to temporarily cover a hole in your roof left by a passing tornado? Does your family know how to evacuate from the house should a fire break out? Do you have fire extinguishers present and do you know how to deploy them? These are all skills that cost little or nothing other than a bit time and focus to obtain.

When it comes to the topic of personal safety, do you have the knowledge and ability to defend yourself? Far too many people purchase a weapon of some sort and then never take the time to learn to use it. A gun, knife, or can of mace is not a magic wand that will send an attacker fleeing in fear. Make sure that whatever self-defense item that you decide to employ is legal in your state and that you have been properly trained not only in its usage, but also in scenarios that are legally allowed for its deployment.

As you can surely now see, the functional aspect of prepping is where the rubber truly meets the road. I would encourage each reader to make a few lists of where they need to increase their knowledge base. Every person's needs will differ slightly, but I would concentrate on these main areas: home, car, first aid, shelter, personal safety. Based on your location and lifestyle, try to anticipate what kind of emergency situations may be most likely to happen. Read the owner's manual for your vehicles, especially the one you designate as the family bug out vehicle. Ensure that everyone in your household who is of driving age is competent in operating the vehicle, should you become separated or incapacitated in some way. As with most things in life, a little bit of preparation in advance will often times pay off greatly down the road. You may never need to set a broken bone while in the backwoods or filter water from a mud hole, but you very well may need to change a flat tire on the way home or put out a grease fire in your kitchen. You never know what emergency may rise up at any given time. Don't let a lack of knowledge keep you from using all that nice gear you've purchased to respond to it.

Also, don't feel like you need to keep all of this knowledge just in the grey matter between your ears. If it helps, keep a notebook handy to make notes of how to perform certain tasks. You may find that you fill it up quickly and it becomes a valuable part of your prepping gear. In addition, learn from those already in the field who have been there and done that, and learned the lessons that failure so readily teaches. To paraphrase an old saying, "a man might learn from his own mistakes, but the wise man learns from the mistakes of others."

Chapter 3: Physical Preparedness

Gun guys have a running joke amongst their circles about the individual known as the "mall ninja." This character is pretty much the same the world over. They are equipped with the latest, most expensive gear. They are decked out in military garb. They loudly tell wondrous, harrowing tales of their time spent with the most clandestine Special Forces teams. They brag of their prowess with all manner of weaponry. In short, these guys are true gods of war. However, outside of their own delusional fantasies, most of these guys are not soldiers, exhibit a frightening lack of common sense around firearms, and are not, shall we say, at their "fighting weight." In other words, when the apocalypse hits, the likelihood of them making it past the end of their driveway, while loaded down with gear and weaponry, without having a heart attack, is quite slim indeed. They too have fallen victim to the "gear before everything else" mentality.

Most of us, prepper or not, know that physical fitness is a vital part of living a healthy life. And, I will admit, I hate going to the doctor for my annual physical as much as the next guy, but the fact that I have a wife and two children depending on me is all the motivation I need to make that appointment. I've always been the type that refused to go to the doctor unless something was broken or bleeding profusely, but as I get older, I can definitely see the merit in keeping ahead of any potential medical issues. Not only can I put a stop to them before they get bad, but it will also benefit me financially by not having to pay for treatments and / or maintenance medication down the road.

The seasoned prepper knows the importance of being physically fit. The romanticized view that many new preppers have is that of society collapsing behind them as they shoulder their INCH (I'm not coming home) bag and head off to the hills, where Mother Nature will provide everything they need. All too often, most of us would wind up the same as the mall ninja example: winded and wheezing by the time we hit the mailbox.

Now, being physically fit doesn't mean that you need to run out and purchase a gym membership and clean out the nutritional supplements aisle at the grocery store. Once you've determined that your shape is more round than it should be, it's time for that dreaded trip to the doctor. He or she will be able to run bloodwork and other tests to determine just how out of shape you are. It's possible that you have good genes and, other than required weight loss, you are in fairly good overall health. It's also possible that you may have several issues going on, each needing to be addressed in the near future. You don't want to make your condition worse by jumping the gun on an exercise and diet program that do more harm than good.

Assuming no major issues are found, you and your doctor should be able to work out a fairly straight forward exercise and dietary plan. It's doubtful that the red-haired clown at the golden arches will play a large role in your wellness plan, so cutting out the fast food now will definitely be beneficial. Dropping the sugary sodas will also help to start conditioning your body to a healthier balance, as the caffeine in them is addictive. Yes, you will likely experience withdrawal headaches, but they do subside in time as your body gets used to a higher intake of water and a lower intake of artificial colors and sweeteners. And you know I'm going to say it, so just prepare yourself: the tobacco and nicotine has got to go as well. Not only are they detrimental to your body, but better you wean yourself now while times are good than to wait until the grid is down and those products are no longer attainable. Conditions in a society experiencing a true SHTF situation are not conducive to a 12 step system to quit cigarettes.

At this point, you need to be incorporating exercise into your daily or weekly routine. The level of intensity can vary depending on your starting health conditions, and can be as simple as a daily walk or as intense as 2 hours daily at the gym. The level of intensity is entirely up to you and your abilities, but keep in mind your overall goal. In a grid down situation, you may be doing a lot of walking. Cardio endurance training may be the ticket to prepare for this, along with weight lifting worked in, considering the fact that all of your worldly possessions may be in a bag on your back. Even if the apocalypse never occurs to that level, being in shape is always going to pay dividends in the long run.

While it may be a pain in the butt to get accustomed to this new life of wellness, you must keep in mind the benefits of this lifestyle to the committed prepper. First of all, a healthy lifestyle will reduce your excess weight, which will lead to increased endurance. We've all seen the stories of people who have lost tremendous amounts of weight and gone on to do incredible things like running marathons, climbing mountains, etc. Many of them could do nothing more than walk a few hundred feet in the beginning before becoming exhausted. However, once the weight began to fall off, their endurance increased steadily to the point where short walks become long walks, and eventually walking became running. Cutting out the junk food and cigarettes will also help exponentially in this department. Once you start losing the gut and gaining back lung capacity, your body may very well be capable of doing things you haven't been able to do since you were a kid. There is no downside to increasing your level of endurance. Whether you are fleeing town on foot to escape some form of chaos or simply wanting to be able to hike with your family for an afternoon, endurance will be the deciding factor in whether you can take part and survive the experience or simply have to sit on the sidelines.

Another aspect of a healthy lifestyle is that of flexibility. Once you begin to exercise and stretch, the results can truly be life changing. When you strengthen your muscles and begin to increase your flexibility, you help reduce the chances of injury due to overexertion. We all know how sore and painful the day after a long workout or period of physical exertion can be. However, the best way to move beyond that pain is to get moving again. Exercise sessions such as yoga classes (yes, guys can do it too) can begin to condition those joints and muscles to be able to flex the way they could when you were climbing trees as a kid. It takes time and effort, but the payoff is definitely worth it.

Good health will also help to increase your body's natural immunity level. When your body is healthy, you can more efficiently fight off infection and sickness. There's a reason that older people are always more affected by a serious illness such as the flu and pneumonia: their immune systems are in a weakened condition, and therefore cannot fight off the sickness as efficiently as they once could. In an SHTF situation, or even in the aftermath of a localized natural disaster, conditions may be hazardous. In the aftermath of Hurricane Katrina, New Orleans and the surrounding area was inundated by vast amounts of toxic sewage and other industrial hazards. Even the water flooding the streets was dangerous to exposed skin, as all manner of contaminants were mixed into it, creating a toxic brew. In these types of situations, having an immune system that is in top notch condition could mean the difference between surviving and suffering a miserable prolonged illness due to exposure to some nasty bacteria or toxin.

Yet another benefit to maintaining a healthy lifestyle is that as one becomes more physically fit, there is often a reduction or elimination of some types of maintenance medications. I've seen family members who were on more maintenance medications than I can count slowly start to wean themselves off as they began to get back into shape. Medications for conditions such as high blood pressure, high cholesterol, and diabetes may be able to be reduced, and in a lot of cases, eliminated altogether due to transitioning to a more healthy and active lifestyle. Consider a scenario where all the supply lines have stopped and the local pharmacy has been emptied. What will you do if you are dependent on these types of medications? Just as an apocalyptic event is not the time to figure out how to use your gear, it is also not the time for you to figure out that you have to make major life changes fast in order to survive without those prescription maintenance medications. Physical fitness will certainly not negate the need for all drugs, but it can definitely eliminate the need for some. In cases where a maintenance drug is not likely to ever be unnecessary, I would heartily encourage the user to take advantage of any prescription drug program that allows for a 90 day supply versus the traditional 30 day supply. I know that my health insurance encourages the mail order and delivery of maintenance medications in the 90 day increments, and even offers incentives to take part in this program.

It should be clear now that a healthy lifestyle adopted now will definitely be beneficial for the rest of your life. Healthy foods will supply the nutrients that your mind and body need to function correctly, and once you get adapted to drinking mostly water, you will be better suited to a life without sodas and coffee should the grid go down and those luxuries are no longer available. Exercise will help lean and tone your body, allowing you to be more capable of doing the tasks necessary to survival. The perfect time to start this journey is today, so make that appointment for a physical and get started!

Chapter 4: Financial Preparedness

Most of us who are at least quasi-responsible adults know that life is full of wants and needs, and that our paychecks will only stretch so far. Unlike our financial geniuses in Congress, most of us try to live inside the constraints of our monthly budgets. While this concept is mainly one of personal responsibility, it also extends into the preparedness lifestyle as well.

While most of the prepping books, blogs, etc., concentrate on some type of cataclysmic event that takes us all back to the stone-age, the reality is that there are much more mundane things that can happen to us that rock us from our cozy life. For instance, what happens when you get laid off from your job during a slow season? What if a family member falls seriously ill and requires hospitalization? How many of us have had a vehicle fail at precisely the worst moment possible? What happens when you need financial relief, and you need it fast?

Studies have shown that most American households live paycheck to paycheck. One little bump in the road, and our whole applecart is turned over. While prepping for disasters, social unrest, etc. is a definite focus of the preparedness lifestyle, one must also be ready to weather a financial storm as well.

If you talk to the average guy, prepper or not, he most likely has a car or truck payment, mortgage payment, toy payment (bass boat, motorcycle, etc), insurance payments, monthly utilities, and all the other payments that pop up during the month. Unfortunately, the majority of Americans have very little saved up to carry them through an emergency should that steady paycheck all of a sudden become a thing of the past.

While I've made as many financial mistakes as the next guy, a few years ago, debt got to be a burden that I could no longer bear. So, being a Dave Ramsey nerd (a link to his website and books is in the appendix), I finally got out all the credit cards, cut them up, and decided that debt no longer needed to play a leading role in my life. Now that I am a few years into this lifestyle, I use only my debit card or cash, and my only true debt is my mortgage, which I reduced from a 30-year term to a 20-year term. Things are still tight, and we are still slightly in the "paycheck to paycheck" category, but things are definitely looking much brighter than before.

As with functional and physical preparedness, financial preparedness may seem overwhelming at first. However, if you follow some common sense principles, it's really not that difficult. First of all, sit down and figure up how much you make per month, and how much your costs are (bills, insurance, etc.). You'll likely find that you have a lot of money going into the rabbit hole of eating out, grabbing a coke at the office, etc. Those unbudgeted expenses can be a killer. Cutting out the unnecessary expenditures will equate to a nice monthly raise in a lot of cases.

Next, look at all your payments that are not utilities or rent / mortgage. Most Americans probably have a car payment or two, in addition to several different credit card payments. If one has adopted, or is considering adopting, a lifestyle of preparedness, financial disasters are definitely an area to take very seriously. It's at this point that you need to decide if all those monthly payments on cars, credit cards, etc. are worth it. If you don't lack much on paying off your vehicle, it might be worth it to throw all your efforts and extra money at that payment in order to eliminate it. If you owe a considerable amount of money on it, you may consider selling it, paying off the balance owed, and buying a cheaper (Dave Ramsey refers to these as a "beater") car or truck. While it won't be the most luxurious thing in the world, it will get you to work and back, and you will be saving money at the same time. Imagine if you took a $500 per month car payment (the average American's car payment now) and put it in the bank instead. How quickly could you save up cash and pay off all those credit cards or other payments that have been bogging you down for years?

Dave recommends maintaining a $1000 emergency account to start with, and after all debts but your house are paid off, boosting that to a 3-6 month emergency fund. This would allow you to weather a layoff, job loss, birth of a child, etc. without relying on borrowing any more money. Consider all the luxuries that we all have and love, such as cable or satellite television, cell phone plans, etc. Have you looked at your statement in a while to see if you could save some money monthly? You'd be surprised at how much you might be able to save if you just shopped around a bit. Plus, you might look at that monthly cable bill and determine that it's just not worth it and pull the plug. Internet TV options are becoming cheaper and more numerous by the day, so you may be able to still watch your favorite shows or movies, yet save a ton of money monthly.

Since prepping covers both short and long term contingency plans, how does your retirement plan look? Are you putting away money for those golden years, or are you hoping that the government will take care of you? After getting those debts paid off, Dave recommends putting 15% of your income into retirement. Do that for about 30 years and you will be sitting on a nice little pad so that those golden years are truly enjoyable.

As with other aspects of prepping, consult people in the field who are experts. A competent financial planner can outline several different options for planning both short term and long term. If you have young kids, starting an education fund now would be a smart move, especially with the cost of private schools or a college education. You don't want to be struggling your whole working life just to find that when you are finally ready to retire, there's no money there. Far too many of us stretch ourselves thin just trying to "keep up with the Jones's", when in reality, those we are trying so desperately to impress are up to their eyeballs in debt and their whole perceived "American dream" is nothing more than a house of cards that crumbles upon the arrival of the first financial storm.

Delayed gratification can be a wonderful thing. So, while it may not be pleasant to drive a $1500 beater truck, once those debts are paid off and you have some "rainy day" money in the bank, you can upgrade to a nicer vehicle. Just don't fall for the trap of perpetual debt. Once you are financially free, the sky is the limit. If the economy tanks, consider how ahead of the game you would be if you have a paid-for vehicle and even a house. Plus, think of all the cool gear that you can now purchase and pay for in full, instead of having to worry about the credit card bills showing up at the end of the month.

Chapter 5: Emotional Preparedness

This chapter will deal with the emotional aspect of preparedness. A disaster, be it natural or man-made, is likely to bring out as many different emotional responses as there are people who experienced it. Emotions such as panic, shock, rage, despair, sadness, confusion, and the like will be present and it will be very beneficial to the beginning or seasoned prepper to be able to not only recognize those emotions and reactions, but also be able to take charge of their own emotions and be able to move forward in a positive, productive manner.

Back in April of 2011, my area saw a massive outbreak of tornados. For nearly 24 hours straight, storm after storm spawned multiple tornados that ripped through the surrounding communities. Entire areas were decimated, while houses just down the road were left virtually untouched. In many cases, it just seemed that there was no rhyme or reason to the destruction.

In the small town of Ringgold, Georgia, a tornado touched down that tore straight through the center of town. Social media footage showed shell-shocked residents just wandering the road in the aftermath of the storm like zombies in a movie. They were in utter disbelief of what had just occurred. Other people lay trapped in the rubble, panicking that help would not be able to find them. Others, including first responders and average citizens, jumped into action by clearing debris, treating the wounded, and checking houses for survivors. The same event spawned emotions ranging the whole spectrum.

In my own household, I had two small children who were terrified for the better part of the day. We live at the base of a mountain, and the tornado sirens on top of it wailed many times throughout the day as the storm systems passed over us. My wife and I watched as the sky turned green and all of a sudden debris began falling as a tornado had touched down about 2 miles south of us. We watched in amazement as wood, roofing shingles, insulation, and other construction debris began to litter our street. We knew that the damage had to be substantial. Fortunately, our little neighborhood was spared the brunt of the storm, with only superficial damage sustained. We spent the next few days cleaning up and also volunteered down in Trenton, Georgia with relief efforts. I wanted my children to see the importance of communities pulling together in the aftermath of a devastating storm. It's a lesson they remember to this day.

The emotions of that day also stick with them, especially my son. He's always been scared of stormy weather, and this event truly solidified his fears. Our house does not have a basement, so our only shelter at the time was the small storage closet under our stairs. We laid out sleeping bags and pillows and their bicycle helmets and weathered it out. After seeing the devastation of the community down the road from us, I could see the folly of my plan. Entire homes were ripped from their foundations. Our closet hideaway would have been useless in the face of such a storm. Since that outbreak, I have installed an F5-rated storm shelter in my garage. Not only does it provide physical shelter in the event another system of this magnitude comes through, but it also provides emotional reassurance that there is a room in our house strong enough to withstand the most violent of storms. It's made a difference in my son's outlook whenever the skies begin to darken.

During a disaster, be it natural or something man-made, it's important to remain calm and in control of yourself. I know that may be easier said than done, but if you can remain level-headed, you are better equipped to assist those around you who may be in shock or in hysterical panic. People in high stress situations, such as soldiers, law enforcement, and first responders, are taught to compartmentalize their emotions. In essence, they have to put all emotions aside and deal with the problem at hand. Once the event is over, they can process everything they feel about the event. This is how soldiers can storm a battlefield in the face of massive resistance. It's also how the EMS worker can treat an infant who is the victim of domestic violence. All of the rage, fear, anger, and sadness that may be associated with these situations is temporarily put on hold, and business is taken care of. Afterwards, some people need to talk with counselors or clergy in order to make sense of it all. Others find that quiet contemplation helps them deal with it. Still others find additional outlets such as exercise, yoga, artistic expression, etc., to let out the emotions that they have repressed during this time. The bottom line is that you must be in charge of your own emotional state during a time of upheaval, especially if you have children or a spouse depending on you to be their firm foundation at the time.

When it comes to a natural disaster, keeping calm and getting yourself and loved ones to shelter is your top priority. That can be difficult with kids crying, spouses yelling, etc., but you have to put all that aside and tackle the problem at hand. Once the event is over, you may have to be a voice of reassurance that everything will be OK, especially if there was substantial damage or loss as a result of the disaster. In the event that you evacuated an area, you might return to complete devastation. Again, this is when being that firm foundation will be an essential skill. Loved ones, especially children, will have a hard time processing the loss of a home, so the ability to answer the same questions repeatedly or to just simply be a shoulder to cry on will be a required skill set.

In the event of a man-made disaster, the immediate goal is also to get yourself and your loved ones to a secure location. Events such as the Boston Marathon bombing happened in public and exposed all segments of society, including children, to a horrific scene where there was much gore as a result of the explosions. In cases such as this, once everyone is secure, you would do well to minimize younger ones' exposure to the worst of the violence. Distraction and moving away from the scene will be your best bet. There may be lots of questions that come later, such as why this happened, why are people mean, and why did they do this to us? Just as in a natural disaster, you have to be that calm, steady sense of normalcy. You likely won't have all the answers, but consistent reassurance will help minimize the long-term emotional effects.

If you are the type of person that readily displays emotion, the concept of putting it all away until the event is over may be a difficult one to master. There are lots of resources available that deal with this subject, and some are listed in the appendix section of this book. I would recommend researching the subject and reading up on topics such as compartmentalization, fight versus flight, and the effects of shock on the human body and mind. Knowing that the feelings you are experiencing are a natural, biological process can bring a level of reassurance that you are not crazy or out of control. Being grounded internally will help you weather a disaster without completely losing control or focus. The more grounded and in control of yourself you are, the more of an asset you will be during turbulent times.

So, now that you've made it through an event, what do you do with the emotions that come flooding back once a little bit of time has passed? Once again, that depends on your individual personality and how you process emotions. Some people, like soldiers who have returned from war zones, may suffer the effects of PTSD (Post-Traumatic Stress Disorder). This can manifest itself in many ways, such as depression, aggression, recurring nightmares, paranoia, etc. This is the most severe type of emotional trauma, and likely will require professional counseling, or at the minimum, a very loving and committed support system to be able to lean on at a moment's notice. It's far from unmanly to ask for help if someone has experienced this type of trauma. Law Enforcement, EMS, and firefighters experience this phenomenon as well. They see the worst that humanity has to offer, and part of their job is to deal with all they see in the most healthy manner possible. In a disaster situation, you may all of a sudden be thrust into the same category. Death, destruction, and sadness may result after a massive tornado rips through a town. It's at this point that it's time to saddle up and do what's necessary to get through the immediate aftermath. In the days and weeks that follow, it's just as important to allow those thoughts, feelings, and emotions to vent as they arise. Keeping these things repressed will only deepen their impact.

While not all natural disasters or man-made events will have the same psychological impact, it's important to understand that in these events, one's emotional and physical well-being may be pushed to their limits. In a complete societal collapse where there is no longer rule of law, it may be up to you to defend yourself or your loved ones against people who are ready and willing to take what you have, and have absolutely zero hesitation in harming or killing you to do so. Are you mentally and emotionally prepared to do what it takes to defend yourself or your loved ones, even if that involves harming others or taking another human's life? While (hopefully) the chances of having to do so are slim, it's easy to see in other countries that have seen an economic or societal meltdown that it doesn't take long until law and order are a thing of the past and violence rules the streets. Better to mentally play through the ramifications, even if an event like this never comes to pass.

It's important to have a handle on as much as possible before something occurs. While not all possibilities can be planned for, there are some basic questions that you can ask of yourself that will help you be ready to weather a very emotional period of time, be it brief or protracted.

First of all, have some sort of idea of what your breaking point is. Most of us have hit this point at some time in our lives. It's when we simply cannot handle anything else, and need to escape from the situation. During a disaster or emergency situation, adrenaline and other chemicals will activate in the brain, allowing most of us to push past the initial confusion that takes over when normal life suddenly spirals out of control. It's during this time that we determine our response to the fight or flight scenario. Once engaged, our ability to compartmentalize will help the majority of us do what needs to be done. However, at some point, the adrenaline rush fades, and other feelings, such as exhaustion, sadness, anger, etc., begin to creep in. This is when knowing your breaking point is vital. When you recognize that you are rapidly approaching that point, it's time to step away if at all possible. Get away from the situation and take a few minutes to breathe and decompress. Often times, this will allow you to find your center and get back into the ballgame. For each of us, this point is different. Some people simply cannot bear much in a disaster situation. For people like this, the best way to deal with the situation is from the sidelines. For those who have a high tolerance for the unexpected, they will be the ones to rush into action. There is no right or wrong here, and in some cases, you may very well not know what your reaction will be until an event arises. Some people who think they can weather any storm will suddenly crumble at the sight of a severely wounded person. Others who seem to be the meekest of all may suddenly and heroically rise to the occasion. I think of Desmond Doss, who was the focal point of the recent movie *Heartbreak Ridge*.

Doss was a conscientious objector during World War 2, yet still sought to serve his country as a medic. In his words, he wanted to save lives, while everyone else was taking them. His faith forbade him to take up a weapon in anger, causing much ridicule during boot camp, as his fellow recruits branded him a coward and a sissy. Fast forward to his deployment into the Pacific Theater, and Doss and his fellow soldiers found themselves tasked with securing a particularly harrowing piece of ground from the Japanese forces. Once the battle began, things got very brutal very fast. Doss's training kicked in, and he compartmentalized the chaos around him as he did his job of patching up wounded men. A hasty retreat found him stuck on the ridge with the wounded and dying. During the heat of battle, he single-handedly lowered scores of men down a sheer cliff, one at a time. Once his commanding officers found out that it was Doss doing this, they began to rally behind him, until all the wounded were extracted. His heroism saved countless lives that day, many of whom were the same ones that gave him a very difficult time in boot camp. Some men who counted themselves warriors crumbled as soon as the bullets started flying, yet Doss rose to the occasion. He credited his deep religious faith as what got him through, as he continually asked "Lord, let me save just one more." Trials will test us all, and some may very well try to push us past our breaking point. Each one of us, prepper or not, needs to realize and recognize what that limit is, and work hard in these situations to not allow ourselves to go past it.

Secondly, it would be advantageous to know what your strengths are. If you are a person who is very compassionate and sympathetic towards others, you may find that your role in an emergency is that of calming people. This role is of vital importance, as people in shock may act in ways that harm themselves or others. Being able to take a terrified person and calm them down is a highly desirable skill in an emergency situation. If you are a go-getter, adrenaline junkie, your role may be as someone who runs towards the danger. You may be the guy digging through rubble trying to pull out someone who is trapped. In another situation, you may be the guy who charges the gunman, disarming him and ending the carnage. Perhaps you are the mentally sharp person who can quickly think on his feet. This type of person can quickly develop a game plan to deal with the situation at hand, hopefully resulting in minimizing the damage and loss of life.

As you can see, this is not an area of prepping that can be dealt with by simply purchasing another piece of gear. It requires that you get to know yourself, inside and out. In doing so, you may very well discover that some of your perceived weaknesses can actually work in your favor. Emotional preparedness is something that we all may need to draw from some day. Be it a major storm destroying a community or an act of terror, our reactions to it will determine our effectiveness in dealing with them. If you are able to keep your emotions in check during the event, deal with what needs to be dealt with, and allow those emotions to come out properly once the event is over, you will be well ahead of the average person on the street.

Chapter 6: Spiritual Preparedness

Many of us who are a part of the prepping lifestyle have probably, at some point over recent years, read the novels written by James Wesley Rawles. If you haven't, I highly recommend them. You can find more info about them in the appendix at the end of this book. In his novels, America and the rest of the world have witnessed a global economic meltdown that has left the nation in turmoil. Power grids are down, law and order is all but gone, and violent gangs seize the opportunity to exploit the situation. While the characters change throughout the novels, there is one common thread among them: their devout religious faith. It's what defines them and it's what ultimately keeps their moral compass functioning, when the whole world around them has descended into chaos and violence.

Just like emotional preparedness is often overlooked, so is the concept of spiritual preparedness. While there are certainly atheist and agnostics in the world of prepping, I would wager to say that the majority of preppers would identify with the Christian faith. While some in the Christian community might argue that prepping is displaying a lack of faith in God's ability to provide for His followers, I tend to take issue with that assertion.

As a matter of fact, the bible has multiple examples of preparedness. Take for instance the story of Noah (Genesis chapter 7). God commanded Noah to take precautions for himself and his family and to build an ark to weather the coming worldwide flood. Noah dutifully obeyed, and proceeded to build the ark. For nearly 100 years, he was ridiculed by those around him, as they scoffed at the idea that such a devastating event would take place. However, when the animals began arriving and entering the ark, I would imagine that their scoffing quickly turned into bewilderment. Noah had positioned food and resources within the ark to sustain its inhabitants, and as the rains began to fall, the bible records that the very hand of God shut the door. As with modern day prepping, the time to get ready is during the good times. The very folks that mocked Noah and his giant ship were now begging and crying to get aboard. It was too late. Their time to prepare was long gone.

Noah isn't the only biblical example of preparation in the bible. In Genesis chapter 41, we see where Joseph, who was sold into slavery by his brothers, has risen to be one of Pharaoh's advisers to interpret the ruler's dreams. The Pharaoh had a series of dreams that Joseph interpreted to represent a coming famine to the region. For seven abundant years, Joseph oversaw the stockpiling of food that was to serve as a reserve for seven years of famine that was to come. In what was probably the largest preparedness initiative to date, Joseph dutifully filled barns and storehouses with the goods necessary to maintain the country through the famine, which came to pass just as expected. In a twist of irony, Joseph's brothers came to Egypt to purchase grain from the very brother they had sold into slavery.

Other verses in the bible tend to illustrate the importance of being prepared. Proverbs 10:41 states that "the wise store up knowledge, but the mouth of a fool invites ruin." Also in the book of Proverbs, chapter 21, verse 20 states that "The wise store up choice foods and oil, but the fool devours all he has." It's clear to see that personal responsibility and preparedness is a virtue that is to be sought after.

This virtue is also not relegated to just the pages of the bible, either. Consider the modern-day lifestyle of members of the Church of Jesus Christ of Latter-day Saints (more commonly referred to as Mormons). Members of this denomination actively maintain up to a year's worth of food and water stores, and encourage member participation in being ready to help one another should a massive emergency occur. In addition to tangible goods, they also encourage debt-free living to ensure that there are as few obstacles as possible to overcome during rough times. If you've never looked into their policies and procedures, I encourage you to do so. I may differ from them on some theological points, but would not hesitate to join in with a network of Mormons for the purpose of surviving a long-term event. For more info, check out the official church website at:

https://www.lds.org/topics/emergency-preparedness?lang=eng&old=true

Spiritual preparedness also encompasses the concept of a person's moral center. For the follower of Christ, the dedication to His teachings and adherence to His lifestyle is of vital importance. To be Christ-like is to be wise, yet humble. Giving, yet prudent. Jesus wanted His followers to be generous and compassionate to all those around them, just as we are to love our neighbors as ourselves and help out whenever possible. However, this does not mean that we are to neglect our families in the process. 1 Timothy 5:8 states that "Anyone who does not provide for their relatives, and especially for their own household, has denied the faith and is worse than an unbeliever." I believe the biblical message is clear: love and help your neighbor, yet your family must always come first. This concept is one that can truly be tested in a time of disaster. It would undoubtedly be difficult to have to turn away a friend in need, but my family comes first. This is not to say we cannot have compassion, but the burden of preparation falls upon each family to ensure that they have what is necessary to weather a storm, be it a natural or man-made disaster. The old adage that "a lack of planning on your part does not constitute an emergency on mine" is very true. This is why we, as a culture, need to truly put a much larger focus on preparedness as a way of life. It worked quite well for our ancestors.

Having spiritual preparedness for me, personally, allows me to know that since I have a personal relationship with Christ, should I die, I believe that I will go to Heaven to spend eternity with Him. This level of faith and boldness is an aspect of my preparedness. It allows me to know that I am willing to do anything that is required of me in order to take care of and defend my family, up to and including death. When one does not fear death, an inner strength is present that may very well be the deciding factor in how one deals with an emergency situation. Hesitation can result in losing precious time that could have been spent escaping or dealing with the situation.

My spiritual preparedness also means that I am a member of a larger group of like-minded individuals, which increases my chances of being able to weather a society-altering event. When you look at religious communities such as the

Amish and Mennonites, their spiritual mantra of minimalism allows them to survive events that barely even disrupt their day to day lives. In a blizzard in Kentucky several years ago, the Amish were the first people to arrive into a community that had been cut off from the main roads. They were able to bring much needed supplies and even beat the National Guard there!

While I am a practicing Christian, I realize that there are other religions as well, most of which teach similar doctrine of kindness to others and personal responsibility. Also, as I mentioned earlier on, there are atheist and agnostic preppers as well. For anyone interested in the preparedness lifestyle, I would urge you to subscribe to some system of foundation and motivation. I am in no way trying to force my own beliefs on anyone, but my faith is who I am, and it is ever-present in my daily life, as well as my plans for the future. My reliance is on God, and I use the brain He blessed me with in order to see that there are dangers in this world, and as the head of my household, it's up to me to make sure that we are ready for them. When you have a spiritual level of preparedness, you will find that you will have that inner peace that allows you to remain calm while others around you panic. Whatever your source of that inner peace is, I would advise you to consider how important it is to strengthen and cultivate it, just as you would a garden. It may just be the very thing that sustains you when society is crumbling all around us.

Chapter 7: You can't be everything, to everyone, every time

There is a certain stigma that many preppers live with, especially if they live in a subdivision or in an urban environment where people know about their lifestyle. The stigma is that of the paranoid militia-type that is just itching to appear on an episode of *Doomsday Preppers*. We all know that while there are some attention-seeking nut-jobs out there, most preppers quietly go about their way, always staying vigilant and ready. In my small neighborhood, the people around me couldn't help but notice when I installed a whole-house generator system and a storm shelter in my garage. Then the jokes started coming....until they needed help. When a severe storm system knocks the power out for more than a few hours, whose house do you think they come knocking at to charge their cell phones and computers? Every time a tornado is a possibility, I have a few neighbors who want to know if they can seek shelter in my safe room in my garage.

Now, I certainly want to be generous and compassionate, but there does come a limit to what I will do for others. Just as in the story of Noah and the flood, people have the opportunity to prepare for themselves and their families in times of calm. Just because they choose not to certainly doesn't mean that I am beholden to them in order for them to survive a grid down situation. When it comes to prepping, the old saying "there's no time like the present" applies perfectly.

While I do build in extra items in my prepping to be able to give out to folks needing help with the basics, I do not consider myself responsible for them in the least. The concept of "give them an inch, and they'll take a mile" is very applicable here as well. When an event occurs, many people (whether they know that you are a prepper, or simply see that you have the fortitude to take charge of a situation) will come to you for help and advice. Some might even expect you to take care of their problems. It's times like these that can quickly become overwhelming.

As you've undoubtedly noticed by now, a common theme in this guide is that you are responsible for your family first, and everyone else second. Times of distress, be they natural or man-made, can often bring out the worst in people. While novels and movies may make it out to be the roving gangs that are the biggest threat, it may very well turn out to be the desperate father with no preparations that may test your limits of compassion. Most grocery stores only carry around a 72-hour supply of food and beverages, so at the first sign of a catastrophic event, they will be virtually picked clean. This means that you either fight your way through a panicked crowd, or you prepare in advance. I prefer to choose the latter. My family grocery shops by the month, minimizing our trips to the store. We also have it delivered straight to our house, where we divide it up into storage totes to make sure that it lasts a full month. At any given time, there is more than enough available in our pantry or totes to last us several days, even without getting into our emergency food supplies. In a short-term situation, this should allow me to help out my immediate friends and neighbors.

In a longer-term situation, things can escalate much quicker. A hungry man may feel forced to take desperate measures, and if he knows you have a stockpile of food, water, and gear, you've just painted a large target on yourself. Being prepared also means that you must be ready to defend your stores. This may mean a stern warning to someone begging for help or may mean conveying your message with a weapon at the ready. In either case, you must be ready to follow through and protect your family. If you've ever fed a stray animal, you know that animal becomes emboldened over time, expecting you to continue what you have started.

So, what do you do to prevent, or at least minimize, an encounter that may turn dangerous? There are a few steps that you can take. First of all, maintain a level of guardedness around your prepping stockpiles and gear. The military refers to this as Operational Security (or OPSEC). Only those in your immediate family and anyone else you deem necessary need to know about your stores and gear. Every time I watch some show about prepping on television, it seems like there is never a shortage of individuals or groups wanting to parade the camera crew around their basement stockpile of weapons, food, and water. I just shake my head and laugh at the fact that they are now some of the most targeted people in their state if something bad ever happens.

Secondly, encourage a basic level of preparedness among your friends and neighbors. A tote full of rice and beans and a few barrels of water are not that expensive or space-consuming to keep somewhere in the house. Perhaps you can host a community first aid clinic to teach the basics of being a first responder in the event of an emergency. During a triage situation, you could easily push yourself past the point of exhaustion if you are the only one present with basic medical skills. Develop relationships with other like-minded individuals so that if an emergency does occur, you already have a network of people to share the burdens of what is to come. In the event that people with ill intentions do come knocking, a neighborhood response team can carry much more weight than an individual home owner.

Finally, be aware of the resources around you that may be able to help out during times of distress. Often times, cities and towns will have a local food bank that distributes food and water to the needy in the community. In addition, many churches have private food pantries and thrift stores to help out people who are down on their luck. Places like this are great to know about, as you can gently, but firmly, refer any unprepared neighbors or travelling refugees to these centers for help, hopefully avoiding an ugly confrontation.

In the end, being an adherent to a preparedness lifestyle may make you feel that you've got to be the hero in any situation. This is natural, as its human nature to want to help those in need. Guilt and coercion can stretch one to the limits, and is something that needs to be planned ahead for before it happens. If you can, stock some extra goods to be given away during times of trouble. If not, know how to say "no" and be ready to deal with the consequences. Be fair and compassionate when possible, but firm when you simply cannot. Remember that it's not up to you to take care of everyone. Sadly, some folks will scoff and ignore the warnings until it's too late, and while tragic, their plight simply is not my problem. I know that sentiment may seem quite callous, but in a long term SHTF situation, it will definitely become a reality.

In closing, it's easy to see that we live in a society where everything we need is as close as our keyboard or nearest big box store. We can dart in on the way home and grab a few things and even wait until the "low fuel" light pops on until we hit the nearest gas station. It's this mentality that has separated us from our ancestors who were the exact polar opposites. Only two or three generations ago for most of us, our relatives maintained a life of relative self-sufficiency, especially in the more rural parts of the country. I have heard family stories of not knowing that the Great Depression had come and gone, because every day was a fight for survival as share croppers or day laborers. Our ancestors knew what it took to survive. We would do well to honor their memory be remembering the lessons that they taught us, and living a life that relies less on technology and "just-in-time" distribution models. At some point, the house of cards will fall. Will you be ready when it does?

Appendix

The following resources are presented to give the reader suggestions on where to go for gear and instruction. I would encourage anyone interested in beginning a lifestyle of preparedness to research any or all of the material referenced here for a good, well-rounded approach to the prepping way of life. Keep in mind that the information presented here is but a small sample of what is available. There are several books referenced as well that will give you a well-rounded prepper's library.

In closing, I hope that this guide has proven useful to you, regardless of your level of prepping. For the beginner, don't let the concept overwhelm you. It can seem like a daunting task, but every journey has to start with one step. You can do it. Just commit yourself to a concept that you, and you alone, are the only one that you can truly count on when disaster strikes. For the seasoned prepper, I hope I've reminded you that there are more aspects to the lifestyle than just gear. To be truly well-rounded, a prepper has to be in control of himself physically, financially, emotionally, and spiritually. It's my sincere hope that we never have to put all these skills to use, but considering the world we live in today, the likelihood seems greater than ever before. Better safe than sorry......

P5 Preparedness

1-423-602-2175

Located in Chattanooga, TN, P5 Preparedness not only offers all the gear that a beginning or seasoned prepper would want or need, they also have classes available weekly and monthly for a variety of prepping topics. If you are in the area, I highly recommend a visit here. Duke and Seth are passionate about the prepping lifestyle and will assist you in getting started.

http://www.p5preparedness.com/

Carolina Readiness Supply

1-828-452-2394

Located in beautiful Waynesville, NC, Carolina Readiness Supply is a one-stop shop for all your prepping needs. In addition to a well-stocked selection of anything from survival food to backpacks, they also promote classes on survival skills and primitive living. At various times throughout the year, you may even spot authors such as William Forstchen of *One Minute After* fame as he drops in to sign books and discuss his work. https://www.carolinareadiness.com/

Emergency Essentials

https://beprepared.com/

This is a website that I have personally ordered quite a bit of gear from. In addition to a massive selection of goods, if you sign up for their email distribution list, you will get daily emails that not only have specials and group buy deals, they also have a very informative blog that covers a myriad of prepper-related topics.

Generac Generators

1-888-GENERAC

http://www.generac.com/

Carrying everything from small portable generators to systems large enough to run a building, Generac is one of the most trusted names in backup power. I personally have one of their 20KW Guardian series whole house generators that keeps us up and going whenever the power goes out. I would encourage any homeowner to consider some sort of backup power system. Mine has been well worth the investment and provides peace of mind when the skies turn stormy. Their products can be found at most Lowes and Home Depot stores.

Fain Storm Shelters

1-888-527-7700

http://fainstormshelters.com/

Our area in northwest Georgia was hit with a massive outbreak of tornadoes in the spring of 2011 and the devastation was incredible. After seeing the damage done to a community less than 2 miles from where I live, I decided to invest in a storm shelter. The good folks at Fain Storm Shelters out of Jackson, TN provided me with a steel safe room that gives my family a sense of comfort when the weather radio goes off and the winds begin to pick up. From concrete shelters to steel safe rooms, they have something for every need and budget. Just like having a generator, a storm shelter is an investment not only in your house, but in your family's peace of mind as well.

Old Grouch's Military Surplus

1-828-627-0361

Located in Clyde, NC, this unique store carries military surplus gear from all over the world. From ALICE packs to surplus clothing, Grouch's is sure to have it. From time to time, they come up with some interesting, limited-supply items, so sign up for their emails and you never know what they are going to offer up for sale.

http://www.oldgrouch.com/

Alan Kay

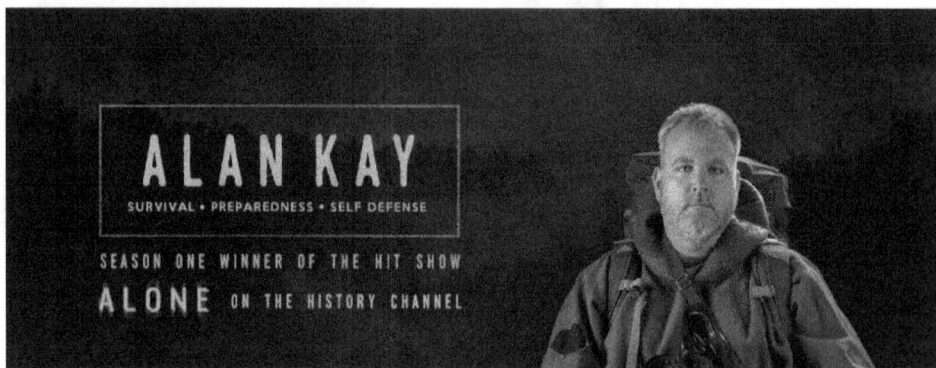

If you are a fan of the History Channel's series *Alone*, this man needs no introduction. Alan is a wealth of knowledge in the areas of wilderness survival, bug out bag preparation, and many other preparedness topics. He teaches workshops ranging from self-defense tactics to survival. I recommend following him on Facebook or Twitter, as well as checking out his You-tube videos (the one he does on his personal bug out bag is wonderful) as well as his website:

http://alankaysurvival.com/

Nicole Apelian

Fans of season 2 of *Alone* will likely recall Nicole as the contestant that maintained the most positive attitude throughout the whole experience. She is a wealth of knowledge on the topics of primitive living and wilderness medicine. If you are able, I highly encourage you to attend one of the various workshops she hosts, as well as checking out her videos on You-tube. I would also follow her on

Facebook and Twitter, as well as checking out her website:

https://www.nicoleapelian.com/

Mike Lowe

Also from season 2, Mike and his fellow instructors at Wilderness Way Adventures offer a unique blend of survival and spiritual training that encourages both self-reliance and a greater understanding of our creator and His handiwork. With classes available throughout the southwest, check out Wilderness Way if you ever have the opportunity. I can assure you it will be time well spent.

https://wildernesswayadventures.com/

Medical / First Aid / Health-related Preparedness Resources

American Red Cross

The American Red Cross offers access to many different classes on subjects ranging from First Aid / CPR certification to Babysitting and Lifeguarding. Simply plug in your location, and the opportunities available to you in your area will pop up.

http://www.redcross.org/ux/take-a-class

CDC (Centers for Disease Control and Prevention)

The CDC website offers a wide array of information on topics ranging from disease identification and prevention to emergency preparedness to healthy living. A thorough reference for those interested in the health-related aspect of preparedness.

https://www.cdc.gov/

Smoking Cessation Resources

Smoking is a habit that is not only deadly, but very costly as well. If you are embracing the preparedness lifestyle, I would encourage you to eliminate this habit from your daily life. Below are some resources to help you on your journey.

https://www.cdc.gov/tobacco/data_statistics/fact_sheets/cessation/quitting/

https://smokingcessationleadership.ucsf.edu/smokers

http://www.webmd.com/smoking-cessation/

http://www.lung.org/stop-smoking/

https://www.smokefree.gov/

Eliminating Caffeine

If you are considering eliminating caffeine from your daily routine, check out the following resources that should be able to help you out and highlight the benefits of being caffeine-free.

https://www.caffeineinformer.com/benefits-quitting-caffeine

http://www.prevention.com/health/quit-caffeine

http://www.artofmanliness.com/2015/09/14/how-to-quit-caffeine/

https://bebrainfit.com/caffeine-addiction/

http://www.livestrong.com/article/482223-what-are-the-benefits-of-caffeine-withdrawal/

Dieting and Exercise

The following resources will help with diet plans and exercise. A healthy and fit body is vital to the preparedness lifestyle. Not only will you be more limber and avoid injury, a healthy immune system will be beneficial if you find yourself in a less-than-sanitary environment.

Diet

http://readynutrition.com/resources/the-bug-out-bag-meal-plan_21032013/

http://www.eatingwell.com/nutrition_health/weight_loss_diet_plans/diet_meal_plans

https://www.nerdfitness.com/blog/healthy-eating/

http://www.healthline.com/health/5-benefits-healthy-habits

http://www.webmd.com/food-recipes/tc/healthy-eating-overview#1

Exercise

https://www.muscleandstrength.com/workout-routines

https://www.exercise.com/workout-plans

https://www.nerdfitness.com/blog/how-to-build-your-own-workout-routine/

http://www.aworkoutroutine.com/

http://www.webmd.com/fitness-exercise/features/workout-routines-ideas#1

Vehicle Maintenance / Preparedness Resources

Keeping your vehicles up and running in an SHTF situation may be something you haven't given much thought to. Also, do you have emergency gear in each vehicle? Do you have full coverage insurance on your bug-out rig? Here are some resources to keep you trucking on down the road safely.

Maintenance Manuals / Diagrams

http://www.chiltondiy.com/

https://www.chiltondiymanuals.com/

https://haynes.com/en-us/car-manuals

http://www.cardiagn.com/

http://www.autozone.com/ignition-tune-up-and-routine-maintenance/repair-manual-vehicle-maintenance

Emergency Gear / Planning

http://www.popularmechanics.com/cars/how-to/g801/the-ultimate-emergency-preparedness-kit-for-your-car/

https://www.ready.gov/car

http://survivalcache.com/emergency-preparedness-emergency-car-kit/

https://www.safetykitsplus.com/

https://survivallife.com/essentials-that-should-car-emergency-preparedness-kit/

Financial Preparedness

Check out the resources below to help you get on the path to financial freedom.

Dave Ramsey

I'm a huge fan of Mr. Ramsey. His method of debt reduction and elimination has been instrumental in turning my own family's finances around. He has numerous books out, as well as live events. Check out his website for more info and details on any events that may come to your town in the near future.

https://www.daveramsey.com/

Clark Howard

Clark Howard is the guru of frugal living. Check out his informative website for tons of ideas to help you save money in your day to day life.

http://clark.com/

Dan Miller

Writer of the best-selling book *48 Days to the Work You Love*, Dan Miller is a motivational speaker who can help you find your passion and very possibly make a living off it. If you are tired of dragging into cubicle-land every Monday through Friday from 8-5, I would highly recommend checking out his website.

http://www.48days.com/

Emotional Preparedness Resources

Below you will find a number of resources to understand the effects of trauma and shock on the human body, and what you can do to minimize their effects and remain in control of yourself during times of trial.

Compartmentalization

https://www.merriam-webster.com/dictionary/compartmentalize

https://www.forbes.com/sites/ryanblair/2012/06/26/5-steps-of-compartmentalization/#6a70841c1a62

https://www.psychologytoday.com/blog/skinny-revisited/201307/compartmentalizing-2

Shock

http://www.medicinenet.com/shock/article.htm

http://www.emedicinehealth.com/shock/article_em.htm

http://www.mayoclinic.org/first-aid/first-aid-shock/basics/art-20056620

PTSD (Post Traumatic Stress Disorder)

https://www.nimh.nih.gov/health/topics/post-traumatic-stress-disorder-ptsd/index.shtml

https://www.ptsd.va.gov/public/ptsd-overview/basics/what-is-ptsd.asp

https://www.adaa.org/understanding-anxiety/posttraumatic-stress-disorder-ptsd

If you are interested in learning more about the effects of warfare and traumatic events on human psychology, I recommend some of the works by Lt. Col. Dave Grossman:

https://www.amazon.com/Killing-Psychological-Cost-Learning-Society/dp/0316040932

https://www.amazon.com/Combat-Psychology-Physiology-Deadly-Conflict/dp/0964920549/ref=pd_sbs_14_t_0?_encoding=UTF8&psc=1&refRID=72H6REE70JE63KCQRKKQ

Emotional Preparedness

http://www.getemergencyprepared.com/forms/emotional.pdf

(The above article is one of the best I've ever read on the subject of emotional preparedness.)

http://learntoprepare.com/2011/06/the-emotional-and-spiritual-component-of-preparedness/

https://foodstorageandbeyond.wordpress.com/2010/06/03/emotional-preparedness-introduction/

http://www.eap4you.com/media/652761/Disaster%20Preparedness%20-%20Being%20Emotionally%20Prepared.pdf

Self-Defense and Preparedness Resources

This section will outline some of the thoughts and methods behind self-defense in an SHTF environment. Your own moral stance on weapons and their usage will determine what is right for your individual situation. Some preppers advocate firearms while others prefer a non-lethal approach such as martial arts, impact weapons, or self-defense sprays such as mace. A practical prepper will always use the continuum of force when dealing with a threat. In other words, drawing a handgun might not be the best way to deal with a suspicious person asking for help. Always be sure to check the legalities of whatever weapon system you choose, and know when it's legal and when it isn't to deploy it.

http://www.theprepperjournal.com/category/self-defense/

http://www.happypreppers.com/self-defense.html

http://preppers-survival-guide.blogspot.com/2013/07/top-10-best-self-defense-weapons.html

http://www.offthegridnews.com/self-defense/a-look-at-alternative-weapons-for-the-prepper/

http://policelink.monster.com/training/articles/9728-six-levels-of-force

http://www.nononsenseselfdefense.com/

http://www.artofmanliness.com/2015/02/05/how-to-develop-the-situational-awareness-of-jason-bourne/

https://besurvival.com/tips-and-tricks/10-ways-to-improve-your-situational-awareness

https://www.stratfor.com/weekly/practical-guide-situational-awareness

Where To Find It In The Bible

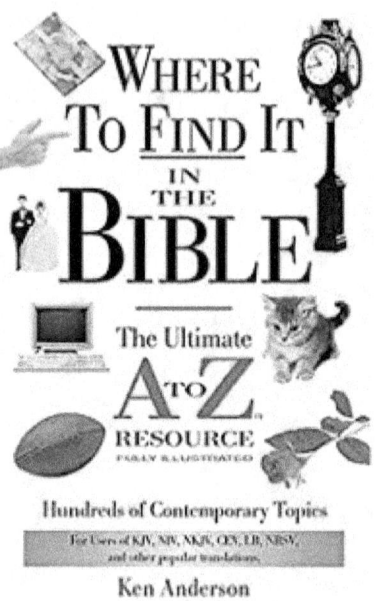

I personally own this book and it comes in very handy when researching what the bible has to say about various topics. The prepper might find the sections on hope, faith, perseverance, wisdom, and preparation very inspiring. This is one book I would definitely have in my library if I wanted to learn more about spiritual preparedness.

https://www.amazon.com/Where-Find-Bible-Ultimate-Contemporary/dp/B010DPVA78/ref=sr_1_6?ie=UTF8&qid=1491336848&sr=8-6&keywords=where+to+find+it+in+the+bible

Here are some excellent articles and websites on the concepts of spiritual and mental preparedness:

http://www.brushfiresmt.com/index_files/Page789.htm

http://www.elijahlist.com/words/display_word.html?ID=13685

http://preparedchristian.net/spiritual-preparedness/#.WOP_iunwvIU

http://readynutrition.com/resources/spiritual-preparedness_29072011/

https://survivalblog.com/spiritual_preparedness_for_hard_times_by_zebo/

Preparedness and Organized Religion

Mormons, as a denomination, incorporate preparedness into their doctrine. Below are several websites and articles detailing their belief system, and the aspiring prepper will likely find some common ground here.

https://www.lds.org/topics/emergency-preparedness?lang=eng&old=true

http://www.mormonnewsroom.org/article/preparedness

http://www.mormonnewsroom.org/article/ted-koppel-mormon-preparedness

http://survivalcache.com/book-review-lds-preparedness-manual/

This article is a little political, but highlights the church's efforts during times of disaster:

http://www.motherjones.com/politics/2007/12/mormons-rescue

Amish and Mennonite Views on Self-Reliance

Most people probably view the Amish and Mennonite communities as just religious throwbacks to an earlier era. However, their model of minimalism and self-reliance could be beneficial to us all. Here are a few websites and articles to read up on.

http://www.offthegridnews.com/how-to-2/off-the-grid-secrets-of-the-amish/

http://www.offthegridnews.com/how-to-2/6-lost-off-grid-lessons-from-the-amish/

http://www.motherearthnews.com/nature-and-environment/sustainable-communities/homestead-heritage-zm0z13jjzcom

https://independentlivingnews.com/2013/11/12/20280-10-self-reliance-tips-from-a-surprising-source/

http://www.survivopedia.com/amish-survival-skills/

Here is a treasure trove of self-reliant tools and gear. It's basically the Walmart store of the Amish lifestyle: https://www.lehmans.com/

Here you will find various books and articles on disaster scenarios, both fictional and real, and how people dealt with / survived them.

One Second After

In this harrowing tale of life after an EMP event, author William Forstchen shows how one small

North Carolina town deals with the after effects and the resulting societal breakdown. There are two additional books in the series. I am a big fan of Mr. Forstchen, and he can be found from time to time doing book signings at Carolina Readiness Supply.

http://www.onesecondafter.com/

Patriots

This novel is the first in a series by James Wesley Rawles about a financial collapse that sweeps the globe and the resulting chaos at home and abroad. Written with characters that you can truly relate to, this book and the ones that follow deserve a spot in any prepper's library. Rawles' website is chock full of information not only about his books, but spans the spectrum on preparedness topics.

https://survivalblog.com/about/

Day By Day Armageddon

I have to admit that I am a zombie junkie, and this series by J.L. Bourne is one of the best. Sometimes we preppers love to think outside of the box and wonder how we would react to a Walking Dead scenario. This series covers the zombie apocalypse from day one in a journal style. If you like zombie apocalypse reading, this is the series for you. If you prefer more reality-based fiction, Bourne has something for you as well:

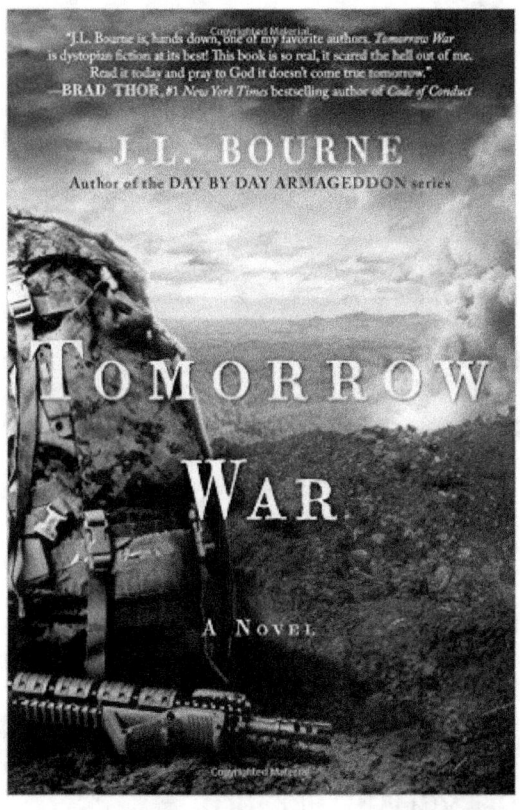

This book, with a recently-released sequel, details the actions of a covert operator that, for reasons unknown to him, bring about a global economic meltdown.

http://jlbourne.com/

Lights Out

In this book, journalist Ted Koppel discusses the vulnerability of the United States electric grid, cyber security, and the danger of an EMP. Written in a very detailed manner, this book shows just how reliant we are on a very attack-prone infrastructure.

http://tedkoppellightsout.com/

The Great Depression

Probably no event in American history has taught us more about the importance of self-reliance and preparedness than the Great Depression. Check out these articles for more about lessons learned from that generation.

http://thesurvivalmom.com/survival-wisdom-great-depression/

http://www.happypreppers.com/Depression.html

http://commonsensehome.com/great-depression-life/

http://www.backdoorsurvival.com/frugal-lessons-from-the-great-depression/

http://www.backdoorsurvival.com/cooking-lessons-from-the-great-depression/

Desmond Doss

With the highly successful movie *Heartbreak Ridge* bringing attention to a relatively unknown country boy, the story of Desmond Doss is an excellent character study into the effects of war on a man and how one's religious beliefs can guide a man through his toughest hours. In addition to the movie, I would recommend the following books about him and his experience.

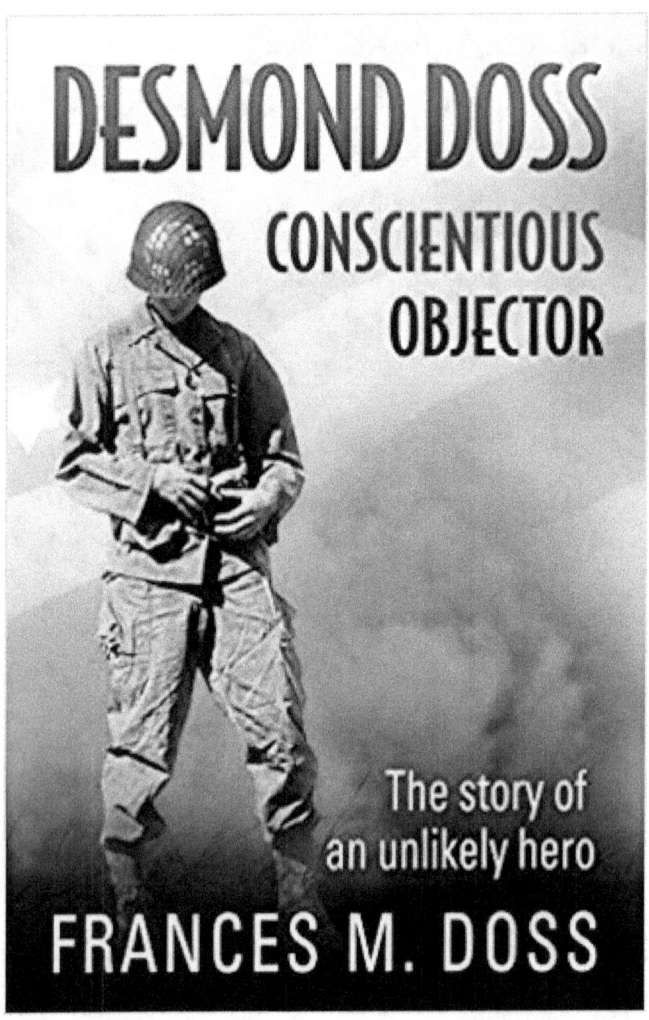

https://www.amazon.com/Desmond-Doss-Conscientious-Objector-Unlikely/dp/0816321248

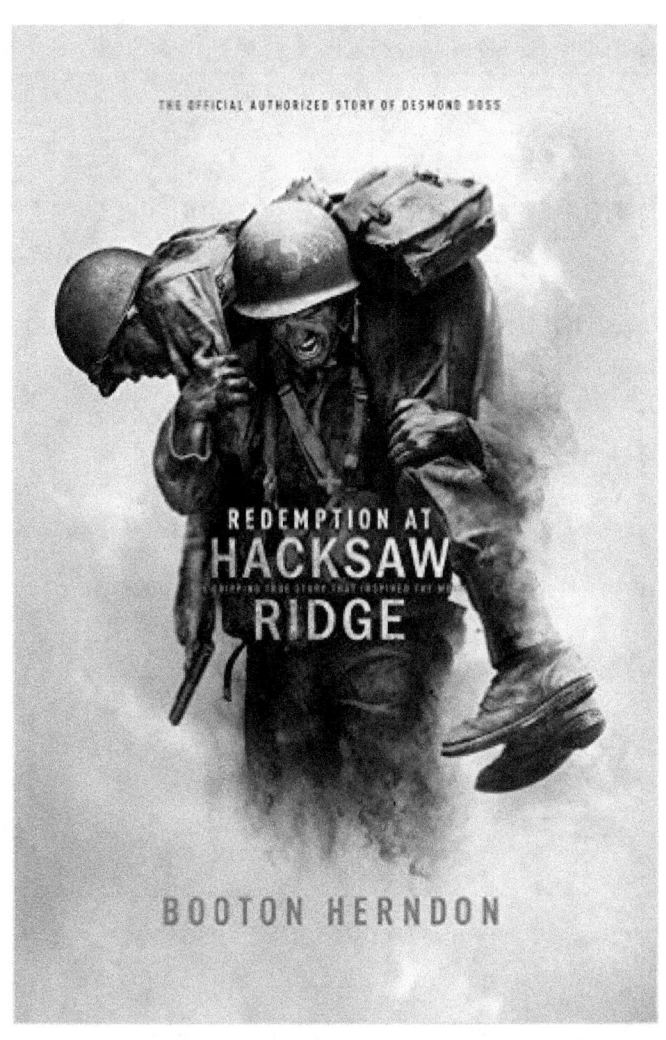

https://www.amazon.com/Redemption-At-Hacksaw-Ridge-Gripping/dp/1629131555/ref=pd_lpo_sbs_14_t_0?_encoding=UTF8&psc=1&refRID=WVJQ2CZQTZ1YEXN2WJ8K

General Preparedness Info

FEMA

In addition to the various resources available on the website, FEMA also offers a free guide on storm shelters, containing various plans on how to construct one.

https://www.fema.gov/

https://www.fema.gov/fema-p-320-taking-shelter-storm-building-safe-room-your-home-or-small-business

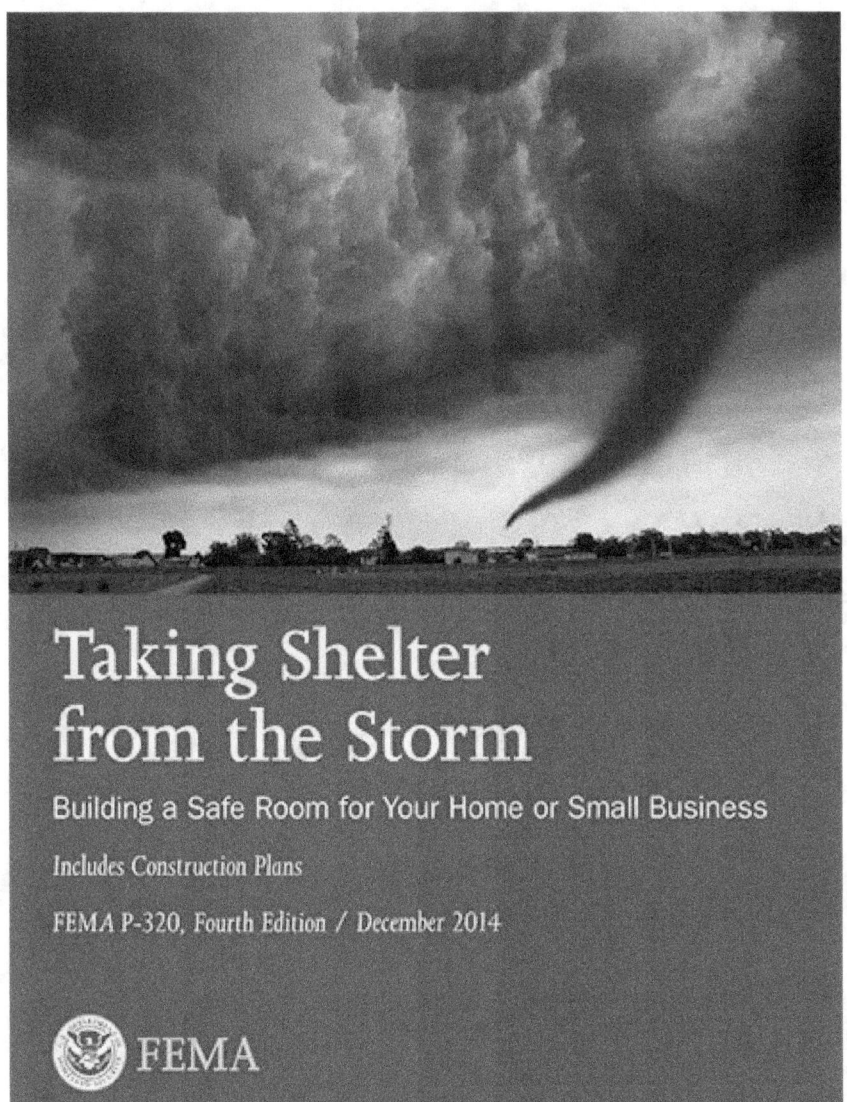

Taking Shelter from the Storm
Building a Safe Room for Your Home or Small Business

Includes Construction Plans

FEMA P-320, Fourth Edition / December 2014

FEMA

C.E.R.T. (Community Emergency Response Teams)

If you are interested in learning more about being a volunteer in your community, check out FEMA's resources on joining a C.E.R.T.

https://www.fema.gov/community-emergency-response-teams

Ready.Gov

Here you will find additional resources regarding home preparedness.

https://www.ready.gov/

Feel free to check out my other books on preparedness topics:

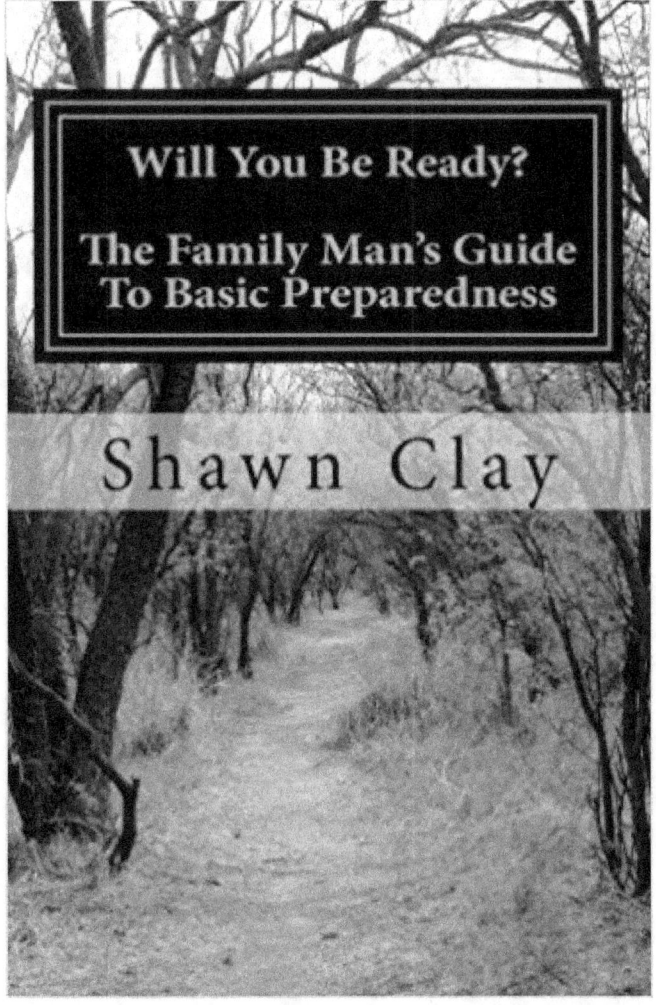

Will You Be Ready?

The Family Man's Guide
To Basic Preparedness

Shawn Clay

This down-to-earth preparedness guide is geared towards husbands and fathers and stresses the importance of being prepared so that your family can safely weather any disaster that comes.

https://www.amazon.com/Will-You-Be-Ready-Preparedness/dp/1537796631/ref=sr_1_7?ie=UTF8&qid=1491512065&sr=8-7&keywords=shawn+clay

This guide will help you when making the decision on what type of storm shelter is best for your situation.

https://www.amazon.com/Refuge-Storm-quick-reference-guide-shelters/dp/154319673X/ref=sr_1_2?ie=UTF8&qid=1491512065&sr=8-2&keywords=shawn+clay

This guide will help you when making the decision on what type of backup generator is best for your situation.

https://www.amazon.com/When-Lights-Out-quick-reference-generator/dp/1543189237/ref=sr_1_3?ie=UTF8&qid=1491512065&sr=8-3&keywords=shawn+clay

Every family has a zombie fan, and this is the perfect book for them. Family-friendly reading on how not to become a mindless walker.

https://www.amazon.com/Zombie-Apocalypse-Comes-Youre-Toast/dp/1537043927/ref=sr_1_1?ie=UTF8&qid=1491512065&sr=8-1&keywords=shawn+clay

Got questions or comments? Feel free to contact me on Facebook (Shawn Clay) or Twitter (@georgiazombies) or shoot me an email at smokey30725@gmail.com.

<u>Notes</u>

Notes